D1123967

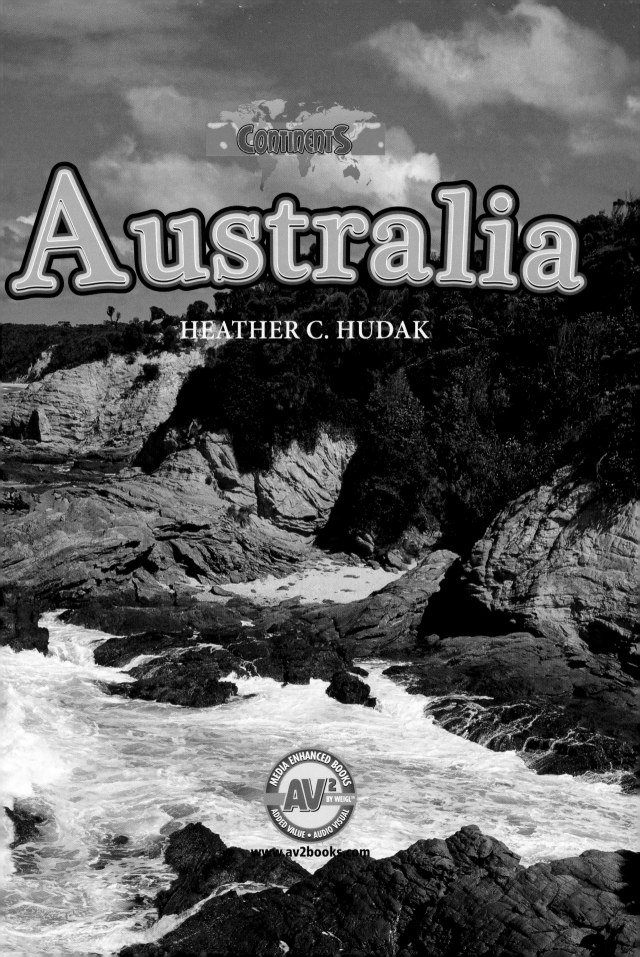

Continents

Australia

HEATHER C. HUDAK

MEDIA ENHANCED BOOKS
AV2 BY WEIGL
ADDED VALUE • AUDIO VISUAL

www.av2books.com

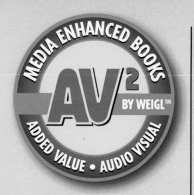

AV² provides enriched content that supplements and complements this book Weigl's AV² books strive to create inspired learning and engage young minds in a total learning experience.

Your AV² Media Enhanced books come alive with...

Audio
Listen to sections of the book read aloud.

Key Words
Study vocabulary, and complete a matching word activity.

Video
Watch informative video clips.

Quizzes
Test your knowledge.

Embedded Weblinks
Gain additional information for research.

Slide Show
View images and captions, and prepare a presentation.

Try This!
Complete activities and hands-on experiments.

... and much, much more!

Go to **www.av2books.com**, and enter this book's unique code.

BOOK CODE

H 8 6 6 7 7 3

AV² by Weigl brings you media enhanced books that support active learning.

Published by AV² by Weigl
350 5ᵗʰ Avenue, 59ᵗʰ Floor
New York, NY 10118
Website: www.av2books.com   www.weigl.com

Copyright 2013 AV² by Weigl
All rights reserved. No part of this publication may be reproduced, stored in a retrieval system, or transmitted in any form or by any means, electronic, mechanical, photocopying, recording, or otherwise, without the prior written permission of the publisher.

Library of Congress Cataloging-in-Publication Data

Hudak, Heather C., 1975-
 Australia / Heather C. Hudak.
    p. cm. -- (Continents)
 Includes index.
 ISBN 978-1-61913-441-6 (hard cover : alk. paper) -- ISBN 978-1-61913-442-3 (soft cover : alk. paper)
 1. Australia--Juvenile literature. I. Title.
 DU96.H83 2013
 994--dc23

                        2011051207

042012
WEP050412

Project Coordinator Karen Durrie
Art Director Terry Paulhus

Photo Credits
Every reasonable effort has been made to trace ownership and to obtain permission to reprint copyright material. The publishers would be pleased to have any errors or omissions brought to their attention so that they may be corrected in subsequent printings.

Weigl acknowledges Getty Images as its primary image supplier for this title.

2   Continents

Australia

Contents

Introduction

An array of natural resources, unique creatures, and scenic landscapes fill Australia. Its coastal waters teem with colorful **coral** and vibrant fish. Australia also has snowcapped mountains, sunny communities, and ancient cultures. Australia is well known for its moderate climate—making the continent a vacation hot spot for tourists from across the globe.

Australia is nicknamed the "land down under" because the entire landmass is located below the **equator**. As the driest inhabited continent on Earth, much of Australia consists of deserts and dry grassland regions. This area is known as the outback. Few people live in the outback. Instead, most of Australia's population live along the southeastern coast of the country, which receives more rainfall than the outback. In addition to its rugged outback, Australia is home to the Great Barrier Reef. This is one of the world's seven natural wonders. The reef, located in the state of Queensland, is the world's largest coral reef.

The Great Barrier Reef off the coast of Queensland is about 500,000 years old.

Many people enjoy diving to view the underwater scenery. The nearby island of Tasmania is separated from Australia by the 149-mile (240-kilometer) stretch of water called the Bass Strait. Tasmania also boasts beautiful landscapes, temperate climates, and relaxing beaches.

Hugh Jackman

Australia has produced some of the world's most famous faces. **Academy Award**-winning actress Nicole Kidman, as well as Heath Ledger, Hugh Jackman, and Naomi Watts, are just some of the Hollywood celebrities who began their careers "down under." One of the world's greatest opera singers, the late Dame Joan Sutherland, was from Australia. Tennis ace Evonne Goolagong Cawley and Aboriginal poet, actress, and author Oodgeroo Noonuccal are just a few of Australia's celebrated artists and athletes.

Kangaroo-tail soup made from authentic **marsupial** meat, and Vegemite sandwich spread, a thick, brown, salty yeast paste flavored with celery and onions, are traditional Australian foods. Such delicacies and snacks can be sampled throughout the island continent in restaurants and supermarkets.

Australia

Australia is 2,000 miles (3,200 km) southeast of Asia and 7,000 miles (11,000 km) southwest of North America. The Timor Sea, Arafura Sea, and the Torres Strait border the country's northern coasts. On the south, the Bass Strait and Indian Ocean border Australia. The Indian Ocean also borders Australia on the west, while the Pacific Ocean creates the eastern border.

Australia is divided into six states. These states are New South Wales, Queensland, South Australia, Tasmania, Victoria, and Western Australia. Australia also has two territories, Australian Capital Territory and Northern Territory.

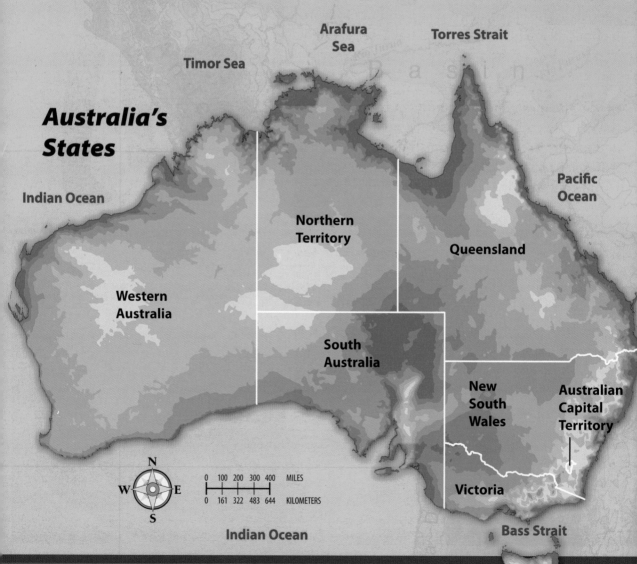

Australia's States

Arafura Sea

Torres Strait

Timor Sea

Indian Ocean

Pacific Ocean

Northern Territory

Queensland

Western Australia

South Australia

New South Wales

Australian Capital Territory

Victoria

N W E S

| 0 | 100 | 200 | 300 | 400 | MILES |
| 0 | 161 | 322 | 483 | 644 | KILOMETERS |

Indian Ocean

Bass Strait

Tasmania

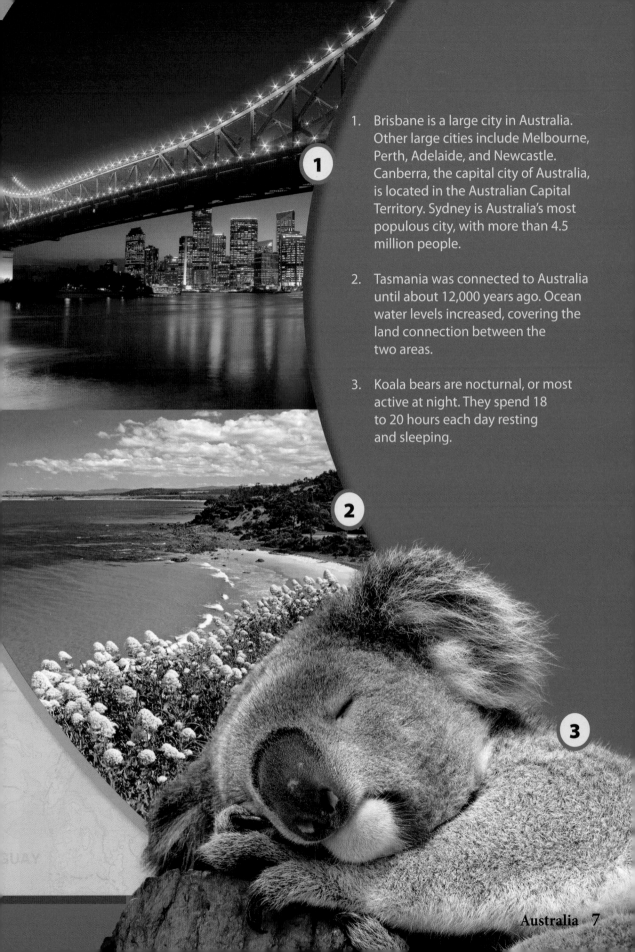

1. Brisbane is a large city in Australia. Other large cities include Melbourne, Perth, Adelaide, and Newcastle. Canberra, the capital city of Australia, is located in the Australian Capital Territory. Sydney is Australia's most populous city, with more than 4.5 million people.

2. Tasmania was connected to Australia until about 12,000 years ago. Ocean water levels increased, covering the land connection between the two areas.

3. Koala bears are nocturnal, or most active at night. They spend 18 to 20 hours each day resting and sleeping.

Land and Climate

Covering about 2,966,150 square miles (7,682,300 square kilometers), Australia is known for its coastal beaches and rugged outback. However, about 90 percent of its land consists of **plains** and **plateaus**. The country is divided into three land regions. These regions are the Eastern Highlands, the Central Lowlands, and the Western Plateau.

Australia's Eastern Highlands consist of high plateaus and low mountain ranges. From northeastern Australia's Cape York Peninsula to Tasmania's south coast, the Eastern Highlands receive the most rainfall of Australia's three regions. The highest areas of Australia are located in this region, as well as low plains, sandy beaches, and rocky cliffs. The Eastern Highlands are also known as the Great Dividing Range because the slopes divide the region's water flow. Australia's Central Lowlands is a flat region where inland riverbeds remain dry, except for rare periods of heavy rainfall. Grass and shrubs cover much of the area, while other parts are a sandy desert.

Dingoes are wild dogs that live in the forests and plains of Australia.

Wineglass Bay is located in Frecinet National Park in Tasmania.

Much of the Western Plateau also consists of flatland. Australia's four major deserts cover a large portion of this area. Grass and shrubs cover some areas. These regions of the Western Plateau are used for grazing land. There are also low mountain ranges.

Two-thirds of Australia's area are located south of the **tropics**, producing warm summers and mild winters. The northern portion of the continent is located in the tropics. This area experiences warm or

hot weather the entire year and has a wet and dry season. Australia is known for minimal rain, clear skies, and large amounts of sunshine.

A monolith is a very large block of stone. Uluru, the world's largest monolith, is located in central Australia.

Get This!

The Australian Alps are located in the southern part of the Eastern Highlands. The Snowy Mountains are the best-known range in the Australian Alps. At 7,310 feet (2,228 m) above sea level, Mount Kosciusko is Australia's highest peak.

There are four deserts in Australia. They cover about one-third of the land.

The Murray River, which is 1,609 miles (2,589 km) long, is Australia's longest river.

Australia's lowest point, Lake Eyre, which lies 52 feet (16 meters) below sea level, is located within the Central Lowlands.

Plants and Animals

O n rare occasions, carpets of colorful wildflowers blanket Australia's deserts. Buried beneath the dry ground, thousands of wildflower species wait for a heavy rainfall before blossoming. Milkmaids, orchids, and honeypots light up Australia's southern regions.

Acacias are some of Australia's most common plants. Nearly 1,000 acacia species live throughout Australia. These strong, brightly flowered shrubs live in nearly every region of the continent. Another common plant is the **eucalyptus**, or gum tree. There are more than 700 eucalyptus species living throughout Australia except in the rain forest regions.

Australia's diverse landscape is home to unique wildlife, including quolls and great white sharks. Marsupials are the best-known Australian animal species. Australia is home to about 150 marsupial species, including kangaroos, koalas, Tasmanian devils, and wombats.

Monotremes, or egg-laying mammals, also live in Australia. There are two types of monotremes: the platypus and the echidna. Bats, rats, mice, and dingoes are other mammals native to Australia.

Desert dragons and flightless birds also roam Australia's land. With about 700 bird species, including the emu, kookaburra, and lyrebird, Australia's bird population is soaring. More than 600 reptile species, including the tuatara, desert death adder, saltwater crocodile, and shingle-backed skink, also live throughout the continent.

Get This!

Australia is home to some of the world's most venomous snakes. The inland Taipan has enough venom in one bite to kill 100 people.

Kangaroo paws are a flower species that is unique to western Australia. Other flower species include the common donkey orchid and the blue leschenaultia.

The Wet Tropics in the northeastern Queensland region is a World Heritage Site. It houses more than 1,160 plant species.

Kangaroo paws bloom in many colors including red, yellow, green, and gold.

The kangaroo population in Australia is about 25 million.

Natural Resources

Australia has many natural resources. About 61 percent of Australia is suitable for farming or ranching. Fifty-eight percent of this land is used for grazing.

Ranching is an important industry. Some ranchers raise beef cattle for meat. As the world's largest wool exporter, Australia boasts many sheep farmers. Wheat, sugarcane, and grapes are some of the few crops that can survive Australia's **arid** climate.

Australia's minerals include copper, gold, lead, and zinc. Australia is the world's leading bauxite producer. The continent also has large amounts of iron ore, nickel, and tungsten. Queensland, New South Wales, and South Australia produce more than 95 percent of the world's opals.

Get This!

Australia produces three types of opal: black, white, and boulder. Most opals come from remote outback deserts. They are made of silica and water, and contain a rainbow of colors.

Sugarcane is Australia's second-largest export crop. Sugarcane grows in Queensland and New South Wales.

Tourism

In Australia, people can **SCUBA** dive through schools of fish and giant clams in the Great Barrier Reef. Thrill-seekers can also venture on a four-wheel drive road trip through the outback. Visitors can take a trip thousands of years back in time, viewing rock art painted by early Aboriginal Australians. Australia is the perfect place to relax barefoot on the beach. Picturesque landscapes, festive celebrations, and a variety of outdoor activities make tourism a major industry in Australia.

Road trips through the rugged outback are popular among tourists.

The Sydney Opera House is one of Australia's most-recognized structures. It is one of the world's leading performing arts centers. The opera house was built in 1973 and offers guided tours twice each week.

The Tasmanian wilderness contains about 3.4 million acres (1.4 million hectares) of rain forest and alpine land. This area is protected as one of the largest conservation reserves in the world. Visitors can see the southern coast from the Hartz Mountains or walk along the shoreline of Australia's deepest lake, Lake St. Clair. For expert hikers, the Overland Track is a must-see attraction.

The Sydney Opera House seats 2,700 guests in its concert hall, 280 people in its performing arts space, and 600 people in each of its foyers.

Uluru, a **sacred** place in Aboriginal culture, is one of Australia's most astounding locations. This huge rock rises from the earth. It can be viewed on a walking, camel, helicopter, or motorcycle tour. Aboriginal Australians prefer visitors not climb Uluru.

The Great Barrier Reef is one of the most diverse plant and animal **ecosystems** in the world. It contains more than 1,500 miles (2,500 km) of coral reef. Visitors can sail around the reef, dive through its clear depths, or snorkel in the water.

Kangaroo Island has pristine beaches, such as Stokes Bay, that are preserved from human development. The Remarkable Rocks stand tall in Flinders Chase National Park. More than 500 years of wind and water erosion created this amazing formation, which looks like huge rock animals, castles, and teeth. Park visitors can camp, kayak, or bushwalk in Antechamber Bay.

At 96 miles (155 km) long and 34 miles (55 km) wide, Kangaroo Island is the third largest island off Australia's coast. The Remarkable Rocks are just one of the many sights on the island.

Industry

Tourism, mining, and agriculture are Australia's main industries. Food processing, household appliances, iron, steel, transportation equipment, and chemicals are also important. Most Australian industries focus on assembly line manufacturing. Factories process goods for export to other countries. Melbourne, Sydney, Brisbane, and Adelaide are Australia's major industrial cities.

Since many of Australia's mineral resources are located in rural areas, roads and railroads provide transportation to these sites. Foreign investors own about 32 percent of Australia's mining industry. They provide funds to pay for new mining communities.

Australia's wood product industries earn more than 23 billion each year. More than 76,000 people work in Australia's forest and wood products industry.

Goods and Services

With industrial growth, low **inflation**, and low interest rates, Australia has one of the world's strongest economies. The last 20 years of the twentieth century were very important in the development of Australia's industry. Even in times of economic decline, Australia has been able to maintain a high standard of living.

Australia maintains a balance of trade with foreign countries. The continent's main exports include metals, minerals, coal, wool, **mutton**, cereals, and beef. Australia imports raw materials for production and manufacturing. Its most important trade partners are Asia and the **Pacific Rim.**

Get This!

Nearly 6 million tourists visit Australia each year, adding $34 billion to the country's gross domestic product.

About 63 percent of Australia's working population has a university degree, diploma, or trade certification.

China is Australia's largest export market.

Shaving a sheep's wool is called shearing. Shearing does not harm the animal. A professional shearer can shave a sheep in less than two minutes.

Indigenous Peoples

Deep in Australia's outback an ancient culture lives according to its cultural traditions. Tales of the Dreamtime and **scarification**, ceremonial dances, and spiritual healers are just a few of the unique rituals and practices of the Aboriginal Australians.

Many **archaeologists** believe Aboriginal Australians traveled from southeast Asia to Australia 50,000 years ago. More than 600 distinct language groups lived on separate tribal lands. Traditionally, Aboriginal Australians were hunter-gatherers. Within their traditional land, Aboriginal Australians often moved seasonally from one place to another in search of animals to hunt for food. When European settlers began arriving in the 1700s, many Aboriginal Australians were killed or displaced from their homes. Today, Aboriginal Australians live in all parts of Australia. Some still live in traditional ways on their own lands.

Aboriginal Australians invented the boomerang. The curved wooden weapon was used for hunting.

Australia has more than 100,000 rock art sites containing images made by Australia's Aboriginal people. Some of the art dates back thousands of years.

The Age of Exploration

Aboriginal Australians inhabited the continent for thousands of years before the first Europeans arrived. In the 1500s, Spanish and Portuguese explorers discovered Papua New Guinea. They believed they had found a previously unknown continent. In 1606, Portuguese seafarer Luis Vaez de Torres proved that Papua New Guinea was an island, not a continent. De Torres sailed through the 93-mile (150-km) body of water between Papua New Guinea and Australia. This body of water was named the Torres Strait in honor of its first European navigator. That same year, Dutch explorer Willem Jansz reached the northern coast of Australia. He believed he was exploring Papua New Guinea's coast, but he had actually reached Cape York Peninsula in northeastern Australia.

In 1642, Dutch explorer Abel Tasman sailed around parts of Australia. Tasman visited a nearby landmass, which he named Van Diemen's Land. Anthony van Diemen was the **governor general** of the Dutch East India Company. This company paid for Tasman's voyage. In 1856, the land was renamed Tasmania in honor of its first European explorer.

British explorer Captain James Cook claimed the Australian continent for Great Britain in 1770. He named the land New South Wales. Cook was the first explorer to reach and explore Australia's eastern coast.

In 1860, police investigator Robert O'Hara Burke and surveyor William John Wills explored Australia. They became the first Europeans to find a south-to-north route across Australia. The pair died of starvation on the return trip.

Get This!

Torres Strait Islanders are the indigenous peoples of the Torres Strait Islands in Queensland.

Aboriginal Australians invented the boomerang. This is a curved throwing stick that, when thrown, returns to the thrower.

Some Aboriginal Australian groups make didgeridoos, a traditional instrument, from trees that have been hollowed out by termites.

Indigenous Hawai'ians killed Captain Cook during his third voyage to the South Pacific in 1779.

Early Settlers

For more than 180 years, many explorers sailed to New South Wales. They charted the land and claimed it for Great Britain. Still, they did not settle on the land. In 1788, British explorer Arthur Phillip built New South Wales's first permanent settlement. Phillip set sail from Portsmouth, Great Britain, on May 13, 1787, with eleven ships carrying more than 1,400 people. Nearly half of the settlers on Phillip's voyage were prisoners. They arrived in Botany Bay on January 18, 1788. A few days later, on January 26, the ships sailed to Port Jackson, where the settlers built a **colony.** This settlement is now called Sydney.

The practice of shipping prisoners overseas was called transportation. Few of these prisoners had farming or construction experience. Their lack of farming experience combined with poor soil made it difficult for the **penal colony** to succeed. There was a severe food shortage. In the early 1790s, two more fleets of prisoners were transported to New South Wales before the first settlers who were not prisoners arrived in 1792. Prisoners were transported to establish settlements in other parts of the continent, as well.

The prison colony at Port Arthur, Tasmania, saw more than 12,500 convicts serve sentences between 1830 and 1877.

Hobart, Tasmania, was first settled in 1803. In 1829, a settlement of convicts was established along the Brisbane River. This settlement became the city of Brisbane, the capital of Queensland. Captain James Stirling led a group of free settlers to build a colony along the Swan River in 1829. Located in Western Australia, this settlement became known as Perth. Additional settlements were built at Port Phillip Bay in 1835 and Gulf St. Vincent in 1836. Today, Port Phillip is known as Melbourne. The Gulf of St. Vincent is now Adelaide. The capital cities of all of Australia's states are built at the locations of the original settlements in these areas.

Between the 1820s and 1880s, free, democratic colonies developed across the continent. Throughout the 1800s, New South Wales developed as six separate colonies. Each colony had its own government system and laws. In 1901, the colonies united to form the country of Australia.

In 1804, British settlers sailed into Sullivan's Cove in Hobart, Tasmania.

Population

About 7.1 million people live in New South Wales—more than any other Australian state.

Forty-three percent of the Australian population lived in rural areas in 1911. By 1976, the population in these areas dropped to 14 percent.

Australia's population has grown tremendously since its beginnings as a penal colony of about 1,500 people. More than 22,000,000 people live in the country. However, Australia has one of the lowest **population densities** on Earth, with 2.9 people per 0.39 square miles (1 sq km) of land.

Few people live in rural Australia. Most people live in the southeastern part of the continent, where there are moderate climates and large rainfalls. About 68 percent of Australia's population live in cities. Southeastern Queensland is Australia's fastest-growing region according to population.

Most Australians are of European **ancestry**. Aboriginal Australians account for only about 2.5 percent of the population. Until the 1990s, most of Australia's **immigrants** came from Great Britain and Ireland. After World War II, the Australian government encouraged Europeans who were homeless due to the fighting to move to the island continent. Many of these immigrants came from Greece, Italy, Yugoslavia, West Germany, and the Netherlands. In the 1970s, the number of Southeast Asian immigrants also increased. About 25 percent of the Australian population was born on a different continent.

The city of Gold Coast in Southeast Queensland is home to about 515,000 people. It grows by 13,000 to 16,000 people per year.

Politics and Government

Many countries on the Australian continent have a democratic government that is modeled after the British government. The British government is based on a written **constitution**. The constitution divides the government into three parts: the legislature, the executive, and the judiciary, or High Court. The legislature, or parliament, makes laws. The executive puts the laws into practice. The courts uphold the laws.

Most people who run for election belong to a political party. During an election, the party that wins the most seats in the lower house controls the government. The leader of this party is called the prime minister. From the elected members of both houses of parliament, a group is selected to act as ministers. These ministers make up the executive government.

According to the Australian constitution, the federal government makes decisions regarding foreign affairs, trade relations, defense, and immigration policies. Each state or territory has its own government, as well. These governments are responsible for all matters not included in the constitution, such as education and health care. States and territories have their own constitutions they must follow in addition to the Australian constitution. The heads of state governments are called premiers.

Sir Robert Menzies was Australia's longest serving prime minister. He served in this role for 19 years between 1939 and 1941 and 1949 to 1966.

All Australians aged 18 or older must vote. Anyone who does not vote may be fined.

In 1856, Victoria and South Australia states were the first places to use a secret ballot system. Today, this system is called the Australian ballot.

Australia is an independent nation, but Queen Elizabeth II is formally Queen of Australia. She appoints a governor-general to represent her.

Australia's Old Parliament House in Canberra was home to the federal government between 1927 and 1988.

Cultural Groups

Although Australians have traditionally been of British ancestry, people from many other countries move to the continent. Since 1945, more than 6 million people have immigrated to Australia. At first, many people arrived from other parts of Europe. By the 1970s, the number of people emigrating from Southeast Asia increased. People have come to Australia from more than 150 countries around the world. In recent years, most people have come from Great Britain, China, Italy, New Zealand, and India.

Many people from the United Kingdom have made Australia their home.

Canberra, the capital city of Australia, celebrates its cultural communities during the 10-day Multicultural Festival. This annual, city-wide celebration showcases food, entertainment, and exhibits from around the world. Events include an Aboriginal smoking ceremony, Latin Carnivale, Greek Glendi, Celtic Fair, Chinese Lantern Festival, and Pacific Islander Showcase. Many cultural groups, including Greek, Italian, Vietnamese, Korean, and Chinese, live in Sydney. People from these cultures live throughout Sydney, but certain communities cater to each group.

In Melbourne, Chinatown hosts many traditional Chinese festivals and activities throughout the year.

For example, many Asian immigrants live on the city's west side in Cabramatta, or Chinatown. Australia's largest Asian festival, the Lunar New Year celebrations, takes place in Cabramatta. There are fireworks displays, lion dancers, and parades. At the Freedom Plaza, shops and restaurants sell Asian merchandise and food. Large Buddhist temples are located nearby. About 380,000 Chinese migrants live in Australia.

Almost 6 million people born in more than 200 countries lived in Australia by 2011, making up 27 percent of the population. The largest group of residents born overseas are from the United Kingdom, accounting for 1.2 million people. The languages most commonly spoken in Australia are English, Italian, Greek, Cantonese, Arabic, Mandarin, and Vietnamese.

The Chinese New Year, or *xin nian*, is celebrated in Australia with many events, such as parades and dragon boat races.

Get This!

Melbourne's Italian community is one of the city's largest cultural groups.

Italian immigrants first settled in New Italy in New South Wales in the 1880s. Today, the community is home to the New Italy Museum Complex that displays cultural items including photos and stories.

Arts and Entertainment

Australia's arts and entertainment industry receives financial support from the government. The government has funded arts schools and provided **grants** for writers, painters, musicians, and composers.

Touring Australia's cities and towns, Opera Australia is the continent's leading performing arts company. The company performs its regular season in the State Theatre of the Victorian Arts Centre and the Sydney Opera House Opera Theatre. The company performs shows across the country of Australia. Another prominent arts company is the Australian Ballet. With more than 200 shows each year, the company is one of the busiest in the world. The Australian Ballet performs in cities and towns across Australia, as well as at international venues. It celebrated its 50th year in 2012.

The Australian Ballet is a full-ensemble company with talented classical and modern dancers.

Theater productions such as *The Mikado* are performed for audiences at the Sydney Opera House.

Assisting with the development and presentation of orchestral music, Symphony Services International supports six symphonies. These are the Adelaide Symphony Orchestra, Melbourne Symphony, Queensland Orchestra, Sydney Symphony, Tasmanian Symphony Orchestra, and West Australian Symphony Orchestra.

Some of the world's best-known celebrities come from Australia. Although she was born in Hawai'i, Nicole Kidman moved to her parent's hometown of Sydney when she was a toddler. Before making her Hollywood debut in 1989's *Dead Calm*, Kidman starred in many Australian film and television productions. At age 16, she landed her first movie role in the Australian holiday classic *Bush Christmas*. Actress Naomi Watts was born in Great Britain but was raised in Australia. Actor Heath Ledger came from Perth. Hugh Jackman, best known for his role as Wolverine/Logan in the X-Men movies, is from Sydney.

Australia is also home to many talented authors. In 1973, fiction-writer Patrick White won the Nobel Prize for Literature. He was the first Australian to win this award. His best known books include *The Tree of Man*, *Voss*, and *Riders in the Chariot*. In 1964, poet Oodgeroo Noonuccal was the first Aboriginal Australian to publish a poetry book. It is titled *We Are Going*. Noonuccal was a writer, actress, artist, and campaigner for Aboriginal rights.

Naomi Watts has won numerous acting awards, including a Saturn Award in 2006 for her role in *King Kong*.

Sports

With plenty of sunshine and warm days throughout the year, Australia is bustling with sports and recreation activities. From team sports to golf, Australia has a sport to suit every taste. Most large communities have professional and amateur sports teams.

Cricket is one of Australia's most popular sports. The game is played on an oval field with two teams of eleven players. Players use a bat that is round on one side and flat on the other to hit a ball a little larger than a baseball. Games can take several days to play. The Australian national team competes against teams from around the world, including Great Britain, India, and the West Indies.

In cricket, the ball is often bounced once off the ground before it reaches the striker.

Australian rules football, rugby league, and rugby union are three popular Australian sports. Each team has between thirteen and eighteen players depending on the sport. Teams try to score goals by pushing past the opposing team toward a goal on the other end of the playing field. In Australia, these sports involve a great deal of kicking and tackling. The players wear little or no padding to protect them from injury. The Australian versions of the sports are much faster than the American games since there are no huddles or time-outs.

The Australia National Rugby Team, nicknamed the Wallabies, is ranked one of the top teams by the International Rugby Board.

Netball is another popular Australian sport often played by women. Like basketball, netball is played on a court. Instead of baskets, there is a goal with a hoop on each side of the court. Players pass the ball up the court.

Water sports, such as swimming, surfing, rowing, and diving, and SCUBA are also popular in Australia.

Sprinter Cathy Freeman is an important Australian athlete. At the age of 16, she became the first Aboriginal Australian sprinter to win a gold medal at the **Commonwealth Games.** Freeman made history again in Atlanta, Georgia, in 1992, when she became the first Aboriginal Australian track-and-field athlete to represent Australia in the Olympic Games. She took home the silver medal in the 400-meter event in Atlanta. During the opening ceremonies of the 2000 Summer Olympics in Sydney, Australia, Freeman lit the Olympic cauldron. At these Olympics, she won the gold medal in the 400-meter race. This was Australia's 100th Olympic gold medal.

Cathy Freeman retired from competition in 2003. She now runs her own charitable foundation to benefit Aboriginal Australians.

Get This!

More than 12,000 people are rescued each year by Australia's "surf lifesavers."

In rugby, players can only pass the ball backward.

Many Australians enjoy bushwalking. This is similar to hiking and camping in North America.

Mapping Australia

We use many tools to interpret maps and to understand the locations of features like cities, states, lakes, and rivers. The map below has many tools to help interpret information on the map of Australia.

MAP of AUSTRALIA

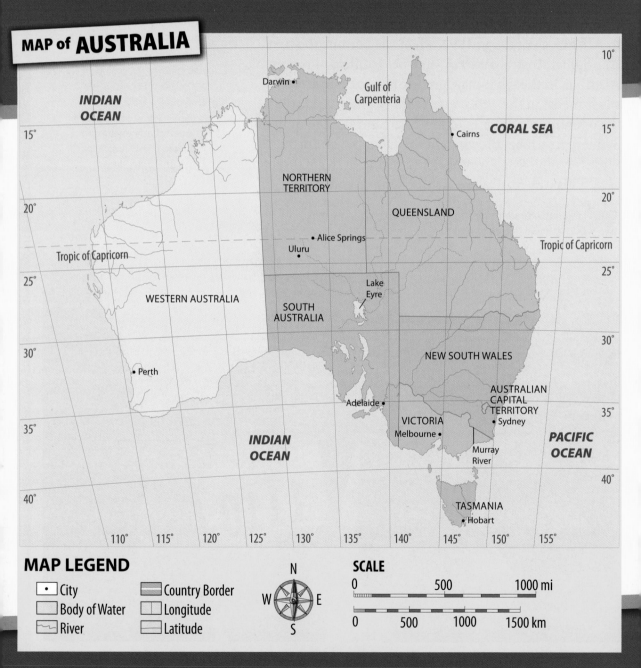

INDIAN OCEAN

Darwin

Gulf of Carpenteria

CORAL SEA

Cairns

15°

NORTHERN TERRITORY

QUEENSLAND

20°

Alice Springs

Uluru

Tropic of Capricorn

Tropic of Capricorn

25°

WESTERN AUSTRALIA

Lake Eyre

SOUTH AUSTRALIA

30°

NEW SOUTH WALES

Perth

AUSTRALIAN CAPITAL TERRITORY

Adelaide

Sydney

35°

VICTORIA

Melbourne

INDIAN OCEAN

PACIFIC OCEAN

Murray River

40°

TASMANIA

Hobart

10°

15°

20°

25°

30°

35°

40°

110° 115° 120° 125° 130° 135° 140° 145° 150° 155°

MAP LEGEND

- • City
- Body of Water
- River
- Country Border
- Longitude
- Latitude

N W E S

SCALE

0   500   1000 mi

0   500   1000   1500 km

Mapping Tools
- The compass rose shows north, south, east, and west. The points in between represent northeast, northwest, southeast, and southwest.
- The map scale shows that the distances on a map represent much longer distances in real life. If you measure the distance between objects on a map, you can use the map scale to calculate the actual distance in miles or kilometers between those two points.

- The lines of latitude and longitude are long lines that appear on maps. The lines of latitude run east to west, and measure how far north or south of the equator a place is located. The lines of longitude run north to south and measure how far east or west of the Prime Meridian a place is located. A location on a map can be found by using the two numbers where latitude and longitude meet. This number is called a coordinate and is written using degrees and direction. For example, the city of Los Angeles would be found at 34°N and 118°W on a map.

Using the map and the appropriate tools, complete the activities below.

Locating with latitude and longitude
1. Which Australian state is found at 30°S and 125°E?
2. What body of water is found at 15°S and 140°E

Distances between points
3. Using the map scale and a ruler, calculate the approximate distance between the cities of Perth and Sydney.
4. Calculate the approximate distance between Brisbane and Hobart.

Where is it?
5. What place is found on the map using the coordinates 37°S and 144°E?
6. Using the map scale to figure out the answer, what landmark is found about 280 miles (about 450 kilometers) from Alice Springs?

Map it yourself
7. Using latitude and longitude lines to guide you, write out coordinates that would meet at any point along the Murray Darling River.
8. Find any two places on the map and calculate the actual distance between them using the map scale.

Quiz Time

Test your knowledge of Australia by answering these questions.

1 Which one of the seven natural wonders of the world is located in Australia?

2 Australia produces 95 percent of the world's supply of this gemstone.

3 Australia is the world's leading exporter of what meat?

4 What is Australia's lowest geographic point?

5 Who were the first group of people living in Australia? How long have they lived there?

6 What is the outback?

7 Name three Australian actors.

8 What is Australia's most popular sport?

9 Australia's government is modeled after what country's system?

10 How many kangaroos live in Australia?

ANSWERS: 1. the Great Barrier Reef **2.** opal **3.** beef **4.** Lake Eyre **5.** Aboriginal Australians; 50,000 years **6.** Australia's rugged, rural interior **7.** Nicole Kidman, Heath Ledger, Naomi Watts, Hugh Jackman **8.** netball **9.** Great Britain **10.** about 25 million

Key Words

Academy Award an annual award recognizing achievement in the motion picture industry

ancestry a person from the past from which a culture or person has descended

archaeologists people who study items from the past to learn more about a culture

arid to lack moisture

bauxite an element in aluminum

colony a community of people who have settled together

Commonwealth Games an event with athletes from the countries of the British Commonwealth competing in various sports

constitution a document containing laws

coral the hard skeleton of tiny sea animals called corals that live in tropical ocean waters

ecosystems plants and animals that are living together in a specific environment and are dependent on each other for survival

equator an imaginary circle around Earth's surface that separates the Northern and Southern Hemispheres

eucalyptus a tall evergreen tree native to Australia, with a strong smelling oil in its leaves

governor general the king's or queen's representative in another country

grants funding

immigrants people who leave one country to live in another

inflation an increase in the price of goods and services

marsupial mammals that carry their young in a pouch on the mother's stomach

mutton meat from adult sheep

Pacific Rim countries and land masses surrounding the Pacific Ocean

penal colony a place of punishment

plains flat, treeless areas

plateaus flat areas of land raised above the surrounding area

population densities the number of people living per unit of area

sacred made holy or worshiped

scarification the act of decorating the body with scars

SCUBA Self Contained Underwater Breathing Apparatus; a container of air used for breathing underwater

tropics the area lying between the points farthest north and south of the equator

Index

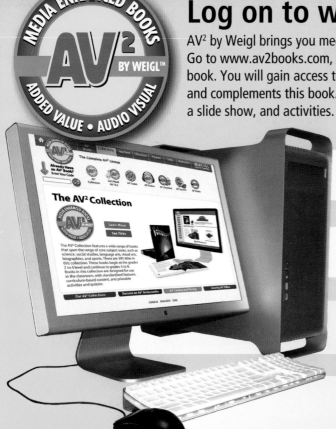

Log on to www.av2books.com

AV² by Weigl brings you media enhanced books that support active learning. Go to www.av2books.com, and enter the special code found on page 2 of this book. You will gain access to enriched and enhanced content that supplements and complements this book. Content includes video, audio, weblinks, quizzes, a slide show, and activities.

Audio
Listen to sections of the book read aloud.

Video
Watch informative video clips.

Embedded Weblinks
Gain additional information for research.

Try This!
Complete activities and hands-on experiments.

WHAT'S ONLINE?

Try This!	**Embedded Weblinks**	**Video**	**EXTRA FEATURES**
Create a timeline of Australia.	Find out more about the land of Australia.	Watch a video about Uluru.	**Audio** Listen to sections of the book read aloud.
Write a biography about a notable person from Australia.	Learn more about a notable person from the history of Australia.	Take a tour of Sydney Harbour.	**Key Words** Study vocabulary, and complete a matching word activity.
Decide where you would go on a trip to Australia.	Find out more about the animals of Australia.		**Slide Show** View images and captions and prepare a presentation.
Completing a matching activity on Australian statistics.	Discover the art of Aboriginal Australians.		**Quizzes** Test your knowledge.

AV² was built to bridge the gap between print and digital. We encourage you to tell us what you like and what you want to see in the future.

Sign up to be an AV² Ambassador at www.av2books.com/ambassador.